CHECKERBOARD BIOGRAPHY LIBRARY

U.S. PRESIDENTS

The United States Presidents

ZACHARY TAYLOR

ABDO Publishing Company

Heidi M.D. Elston

visit us at
www.abdopublishing.com

Published by ABDO Publishing Company, 8000 West 78th Street, Edina, Minnesota 55439.
Copyright © 2009 by Abdo Consulting Group, Inc. International copyrights reserved in all
countries. No part of this book may be reproduced in any form without written permission from the
publisher. The Checkerboard Library™ is a trademark and logo of ABDO Publishing Company.

Printed in the United States.

Cover Photo: Getty Images
Interior Photos: Corbis pp. 5, 21; Getty Images pp. 9, 26, 27, 29; iStockphoto p. 32; Library of
    Congress pp. 14, 20; North Wind pp. 12, 15, 16, 17, 18, 19; Picture History pp. 10, 11, 13, 22,
    23, 25

Editor: BreAnn Rumsch
Art Direction & Cover Design: Neil Klinepier
Interior Design: Jaime Martens

Library of Congress Cataloging-in-Publication Data

Elston, Heidi M. D., 1979-
  Zachary Taylor / Heidi M.D. Elston.
      p. cm. -- (The United States presidents)
  Includes bibliographical references and index.
  ISBN 978-1-60453-475-7
  1. Taylor, Zachary, 1784-1850--Juvenile literature. 2. Presidents--United States--Biography--
Juvenile literature. I. Title.
  E422.E45 2009
  973.6'3092--dc22
  [B]
                              2008035316

CONTENTS

ZACHARY TAYLOR

Zachary Taylor was the twelfth president of the United States. Before becoming president, Taylor had no political experience. He was the first person without previous political experience to become president. Taylor had served his country for 40 years as a soldier. He had proved himself a good and able leader.

Taylor was elected president in 1848. At that time, the United States was growing. Americans were arguing over slavery. Taylor owned more than 100 slaves. But, he did not believe that new states should allow slavery.

Because of his views, Southerners were unhappy with Taylor. They wanted new states to allow slavery. The South began talking about leaving the United States. President Taylor strongly opposed this. He wanted to maintain unity. Taylor never saw the end of the struggle over slavery. He died just 16 months after his **inauguration**.

TIMELINE

1784 - On November 24, Zachary Taylor was born in Orange County, Virginia.

1808 - Taylor joined the U.S. Army as a first lieutenant.

1810 - Taylor married Margaret Mackall Smith; Taylor was promoted to captain.

1819 - Taylor became a lieutenant colonel.

1832 - Taylor fought in the Black Hawk War and won the surrender of Chief Black Hawk.

1837 - Taylor defeated the Seminole Native Americans at Lake Okeechobee, Florida.

1840 - Taylor became the commander at Fort Smith in Arkansas.

1846 - Taylor began fighting in the Mexican War.

1847 - Taylor became an American hero after the battle at Buena Vista; he returned to his Louisiana plantation.

1848 - The Whig Party nominated Taylor to run for president.

1849 - On March 5, Taylor became the twelfth U.S. president.

1850 - The Clayton-Bulwer Treaty was signed on April 19; on July 9, Zachary Taylor died.

DID YOU KNOW?

James Madison was Zachary Taylor's second cousin. Madison served as the fourth president of the United States from 1809 to 1817.

Taylor moved around often as a military man. Because of that, he never voted in any election!

Abraham Lincoln served under Colonel Taylor in the Black Hawk War.

President Taylor took his horse, Old Whitey, with him to the White House. Old Whitey grazed on the White House lawn.

The 1848 presidential election made U.S. history. For the first time, all states voted at the same time.

PRESIDENT OF THE
POTUS
UNITED STATES

YOUNG ZACHARY

Zachary Taylor was born in Orange County, Virginia, on November 24, 1784. He was the third of nine children. Zachary had five brothers and three sisters.

Zachary's parents were Richard Taylor and Sarah Strother Taylor. Both Richard and Sarah came from wealthy families. Richard had been an army officer in the **American Revolution**. Sarah was well educated. She had received her schooling from **tutors**.

In 1785, the Taylor family moved into what is now northern Kentucky. There, Zachary grew up on a plantation in Jefferson County.

The Taylor family was loving. Zachary's brothers and sisters were his close friends. At that time, there were no schools on the frontier. So, the Taylor children studied with a tutor at home. They also received schooling from their parents.

FAST FACTS

BORN - November 24, 1784
WIFE - Margaret Mackall Smith
  (1788–1852)
CHILDREN - 6
POLITICAL PARTY - Whig
AGE AT INAUGURATION - 64
YEARS SERVED - 1849–1850
VICE PRESIDENT - Millard Fillmore
DIED - July 9, 1850, age 65

8

Zachary's birthplace in Virginia

Richard told his children stories about his service in the war. Zachary decided he wanted to be in the military, too. So did most of his brothers. In fact, all but one joined the army. Zachary would later become a famous military hero.

MILITARY FAMILY

In 1808, Taylor joined the U.S. Army as a first lieutenant. He became a captain in 1810. That same year, Taylor met and married Margaret Mackall Smith. Margaret had been born in Calvert County, Maryland, in 1788.

The Taylors had five daughters and one son. Two daughters, Octavia and Margaret, died very young. Their three remaining daughters, Sarah, Ann, and Mary Elizabeth, eventually married military men.

Margaret Taylor

The Taylors' son, Richard, served as a lieutenant general in the **Confederate** army.

Sarah married Jefferson Davis. Sadly, she died just three months after the wedding. Davis later served as president of the Confederate States of America.

Ann married a U.S. Army surgeon named Robert Wood. Wood had served with Taylor in the military. Mary Elizabeth married Colonel William Wallace Bliss. Bliss was Taylor's military aide. He later served as Taylor's secretary during his presidency.

Richard Taylor

A GREAT WAR HERO

During the **War of 1812**, Taylor served at frontier posts in Indiana Territory. There, he defended Fort Harrison. Taylor was rewarded for his bravery with a promotion to major. Then in 1819, he became a lieutenant colonel.

Taylor later served in Wisconsin during the Black Hawk War of 1832. American soldiers defeated Native Americans in this conflict. Taylor won the surrender of Chief Black Hawk. And, the United States received Native American lands in Illinois.

Chief Black Hawk's Native American name is Ma-ka-tai-me-she-kia-kiak.

12

Taylor was a popular and respected military leader. Although he was a high-ranking officer, he wore a plain uniform. And, he often placed himself close to enemy fire. Taylor's men gave him the nickname "Old Rough and Ready."

In 1837, Taylor defeated the Seminole Native Americans at Lake Okeechobee, Florida. Because of this victory, Taylor was made a brigadier general. In 1840, Taylor became commander at Fort Smith in Arkansas. He later commanded Fort Jesup in Louisiana. At this time, he established a home in Baton Rouge, Louisiana.

Old Rough and Ready and his horse, Old Whitey

WAR WITH MEXICO

Meanwhile, tensions between the United States and Mexico were mounting. In 1845, the United States **annexed** Texas and made it a state. This angered Mexico.

Then, the two countries disagreed about Texas's southwestern border. The United States said a river called the Rio Grande served as the boundary. Mexico claimed the boundary was the Nueces River. Both nations prepared for war.

President James K. Polk

In 1846, President James K. Polk sent General Taylor to Texas. Taylor and his men were stationed on the land between the Rio Grande and the Nueces River.

The Mexican War began on May 13. Taylor and his soldiers then entered Mexico. They occupied Matamoros on May 18. On September 24, they captured the city of Monterrey.

Capture of Monterrey

MAP SHOWING THE
TERRITORY ACQUIRED
FROM MEXICO
AS THE RESULT OF
THE MEXICAN WAR

In 1847, President Polk decided to move an army to Veracruz. From there, the United States would attack Mexico City. Polk ordered many of Taylor's men to move to this new position. They were now under the command of Major General Winfield Scott.

The Mexican army learned of the U.S. plans. It decided to attack Taylor at Buena Vista. Taylor's army was outnumbered. But they still won the battle! The victory made Taylor an American hero.

At Buena Vista, Taylor's army numbered about 5,000 men. Still, they defeated between 16,000 and 20,000 Mexican troops.

Mexican and American leaders signed a peace treaty on February 2, 1848. Mexico had to sell the United States thousands of square miles of land. The United States paid $15 million for it.

This land became known as the Mexican Cession. It included today's California, Nevada, and Utah. Parts of Arizona, Colorado, New Mexico, and Wyoming were also included in this deal.

THE ELECTION OF 1848

In 1847, Taylor returned to his Louisiana plantation. The 1848 U.S. presidential election approached. Many Americans thought Taylor should run for president. However, he was not interested in seeking election. Taylor was content to stay home and farm. But, he agreed to run if the nomination was offered to him.

The **Whigs** held their national **convention** in Philadelphia, Pennsylvania, in 1848. They nominated Taylor to run for president. Millard Fillmore of New York was chosen as his **running mate**. The **Democrats** chose Senator Lewis Cass of Michigan to oppose Taylor. His running mate was General William Butler of Kentucky.

Lewis Cass

Millard Fillmore

During the campaign, the expansion of slavery was an important issue. Cass felt that new territories should decide for themselves if they wanted slavery.

Because of Cass's views on slavery, his nomination angered many Northern **Democrats**. They were working to end slavery in America. Many of the unhappy Democrats started a new political party. They called it the **Free-Soil** Party. They chose former president Martin Van Buren to run for president.

Martin Van Buren

Taylor campaigned hard. He reminded voters of his military record. This attracted many Northern voters. Although slavery was a key issue, Taylor rarely expressed his views on this topic. However, he owned more than 100 slaves. This appealed to many Southern voters. Taylor promised that his **administration** would include people from all over America.

In November 1848, Americans voted. Taylor and Fillmore won the election! They received 163 electoral votes, while Cass and Butler won 127. Van Buren received none.

Taylor and Fillmore had won eight slave states and seven free states. Cass and his **running mate** had won seven slave states and eight free states.

FOR PRESIDENT OF THE PEOPLE

ZACHARY TAYLOR

About party creeds let party zealots fight
He cant be wrong whose life is in the right. —

THE TWELFTH PRESIDENT

On March 5, 1849, Taylor was **inaugurated** the twelfth president of the United States. Normally, he would have taken office on March 4. However, Taylor did not want to be inaugurated on a Sunday.

Taylor's greatest accomplishment as president was in foreign affairs. Under President Polk, the United States had gained land on the Pacific Coast. Now, the United States wanted to build a canal across Nicaragua. The waterway would connect the Atlantic and Pacific oceans. Great Britain was also interested in building a canal.

Secretary of State John M. Clayton met with Sir Henry Bulwer of Great Britain. The two men arranged an important treaty. Both countries agreed to keep the canal **neutral** once it was built. The Clayton-Bulwer Treaty was signed on April 19, 1850.

Mary Elizabeth acted as White House hostess while her father was president.

Taylor was the first president elected after the Mexican War.

THE SLAVERY DEBATE CONTINUES

Once he took office, President Taylor voiced his views on slavery. He believed that people in the South should be allowed to keep their slaves. But, he also believed that new states and territories should not allow slavery. Taylor's views did not solve the slavery issue. In fact, more problems appeared.

In 1849, California wanted to join the United States as a free state. President Taylor asked Congress to approve this request. However, some Southern congressmen wanted slavery allowed in California. This started much **debate** in Congress.

Southerners were not happy. Some Southern leaders wanted the South to become a new, separate country. But, President Taylor did not want this. He promised to use force to maintain the United States of America.

PRESIDENT TAYLOR'S CABINET

MARCH 5, 1849–
JULY 9, 1850

STATE – John M. Clayton
TREASURY – William Morris Meredith
WAR – George Washington Crawford

NAVY – William Ballard Preston
ATTORNEY GENERAL – Reverdy Johnson
INTERIOR – Thomas Ewing (from March 8, 1849)

Taylor (center) *and his cabinet*

Many congressmen considered ways to compromise on the slavery issue. On January 29, 1850, Senator Henry Clay of Kentucky presented his ideas to Congress. Clay thought it would be good if some new states allowed slavery.

President Taylor did not support Clay's compromise. He stood firm against new slave states.

Henry Clay

The slavery **debate** continued. Northern and Southern senators argued with each other. Sometimes, fistfights broke out! It seemed the slavery problem would never be solved.

The congressmen who supported compromise would eventually win. However, they would not see victory until Vice President Fillmore became president.

Part of Taylor's annual message to Congress on December 4, 1849

this union has stood unshaken. The patriots who formed it, have long since descended to the grave; yet still it remains the proudest monument to their memory and the object of affection and admiration with every one worthy to bear the American name. In my judgment, its dissolution would be the greatest of Calamities; and to avert that, should be the study of every American. Upon its preservation must depend our own happiness and that of countless generations to come. Whatever danger may threaten it, I shall stand by it and maintain it in its integrity, to the full extent of the obligations imposed and the power conferred upon me by the constitution.

Z. Taylor-

Washington
December 4th 1849.

A SUDDEN DEATH

On July 4, 1850, President Taylor attended a Fourth of July celebration in Washington, D.C. That evening, he became sick. Taylor stayed in bed for five days, but he did not improve. On July 9, President Zachary Taylor died. He was buried near Louisville, Kentucky.

Taylor was in office for only 16 months. Vice President Fillmore became president following Taylor's death. The slavery **debate** continued. Two months later, Senator Clay's ideas about slavery became law. These laws are called the Compromise of 1850.

Taylor served his country for more than 40 years. He was a well-respected, successful, and brave military leader. Taylor proved to be a courageous president as well. He took a firm stand against the spread of slavery in America. Zachary Taylor fought to maintain the United States of America that he loved.

*Taylor was the second president to die in office. He is
buried in the Zachary Taylor National Cemetery.*

OFFICE OF THE PRESIDENT

BRANCHES OF GOVERNMENT

The U.S. government is divided into three branches. They are the executive, legislative, and judicial branches. This division is called a separation of powers. Each branch has some power over the others. This is called a system of checks and balances.

EXECUTIVE BRANCH

The executive branch enforces laws. It is made up of the president, the vice president, and the president's cabinet. The president represents the United States around the world. He or she oversees relations with other countries and signs treaties. The president signs bills into law and appoints officials and federal judges. He or she also leads the military and manages government workers.

LEGISLATIVE BRANCH

The legislative branch makes laws, maintains the military, and regulates trade. It also has the power to declare war. This branch consists of the Senate and the House of Representatives. Together, these two houses make up Congress. Each state has two senators. A state's population determines the number of representatives it has.

JUDICIAL BRANCH

The judicial branch interprets laws. It consists of district courts, courts of appeals, and the Supreme Court. District courts try cases. If a person disagrees with a trial's outcome, he or she may appeal. If the courts of appeals support the ruling, a person may appeal to the Supreme Court. The Supreme Court also makes sure that laws follow the U.S. Constitution.

Qualifications for Office

To be president, a person must meet three requirements. A candidate must be at least 35 years old and a natural-born U.S. citizen. He or she must also have lived in the United States for at least 14 years.

Electoral College

The U.S. presidential election is an indirect election. Voters from each state choose electors to represent them in the Electoral College. The number of electors from each state is based on population. Each elector has one electoral vote. Electors are pledged to cast their vote for the candidate who receives the highest number of popular votes in their state. A candidate must receive the majority of Electoral College votes to win.

Term of Office

Each president may be elected to two four-year terms. Sometimes, a president may only be elected once. This happens if he or she served more than two years of the previous president's term.

The presidential election is held on the Tuesday after the first Monday in November. The president is sworn in on January 20 of the following year. At that time, he or she takes the oath of office:

I do solemnly swear (or affirm) that I will faithfully execute the office of President of the United States, and will to the best of my ability, preserve, protect and defend the Constitution of the United States.

LINE OF SUCCESSION

The Presidential Succession Act of 1947 defines who becomes president if the president cannot serve. The vice president is first in the line of succession. Next are the Speaker of the House and the President Pro Tempore of the Senate. If none of these individuals is able to serve, the office falls to the president's cabinet members. They would take office in the order in which each department was created:

Secretary of State

Secretary of the Treasury

Secretary of Defense

Attorney General

Secretary of the Interior

Secretary of Agriculture

Secretary of Commerce

Secretary of Labor

Secretary of Health and Human Services

Secretary of Housing and Urban Development

Secretary of Transportation

Secretary of Energy

Secretary of Education

Secretary of Veterans Affairs

Secretary of Homeland Security

BENEFITS

- While in office, the president receives a salary of $400,000 each year. He or she lives in the White House and has 24-hour Secret Service protection.

- The president may travel on a Boeing 747 jet called Air Force One. The airplane can accommodate 70 passengers. It has kitchens, a dining room, sleeping areas, and a conference room. It also has fully equipped offices with the latest communications systems. Air Force One can fly halfway around the world before needing to refuel. It can even refuel in flight!

- If the president wishes to travel by car, he or she uses Cadillac One. Cadillac One is a Cadillac Deville. It has been modified with heavy armor and communications systems. The president takes Cadillac One along when visiting other countries if secure transportation will be needed.

- The president also travels on a helicopter called Marine One. Like the presidential car, Marine One accompanies the president when traveling abroad if necessary.

- Sometimes, the president needs to get away and relax with family and friends. Camp David is the official presidential retreat. It is located in the cool, wooded mountains in Maryland. The U.S. Navy maintains the retreat, and the U.S. Marine Corps keeps it secure. The camp offers swimming, tennis, golf, and hiking.

- When the president leaves office, he or she receives Secret Service protection for ten more years. He or she also receives a yearly pension of $191,300 and funding for office space, supplies, and staff.

PRESIDENTS AND THEIR TERMS

PRESIDENT	PARTY	TOOK OFFICE	LEFT OFFICE	TERMS SERVED	VICE PRESIDENT
George Washington	None	April 30, 1789	March 4, 1797	Two	John Adams
John Adams	Federalist	March 4, 1797	March 4, 1801	One	Thomas Jefferson
Thomas Jefferson	Democratic-Republican	March 4, 1801	March 4, 1809	Two	Aaron Burr, George Clinton
James Madison	Democratic-Republican	March 4, 1809	March 4, 1817	Two	George Clinton, Elbridge Gerry
James Monroe	Democratic-Republican	March 4, 1817	March 4, 1825	Two	Daniel D. Tompkins
John Quincy Adams	Democratic-Republican	March 4, 1825	March 4, 1829	One	John C. Calhoun
Andrew Jackson	Democrat	March 4, 1829	March 4, 1837	Two	John C. Calhoun, Martin Van Buren
Martin Van Buren	Democrat	March 4, 1837	March 4, 1841	One	Richard M. Johnson
William H. Harrison	Whig	March 4, 1841	April 4, 1841	Died During First Term	John Tyler
John Tyler	Whig	April 6, 1841	March 4, 1845	Completed Harrison's Term	Office Vacant
James K. Polk	Democrat	March 4, 1845	March 4, 1849	One	George M. Dallas
Zachary Taylor	Whig	March 5, 1849	July 9, 1850	Died During First Term	Millard Fillmore

PRESIDENTS 1–12, 1789–1850

PRESIDENT	PARTY	TOOK OFFICE	LEFT OFFICE	TERMS SERVED	VICE PRESIDENT
Millard Fillmore	Whig	July 10, 1850	March 4, 1853	Completed Taylor's Term	Office Vacant
Franklin Pierce	Democrat	March 4, 1853	March 4, 1857	One	William R.D. King
James Buchanan	Democrat	March 4, 1857	March 4, 1861	One	John C. Breckinridge
Abraham Lincoln	Republican	March 4, 1861	April 15, 1865	Served One Term, Died During Second Term	Hannibal Hamlin, Andrew Johnson
Andrew Johnson	Democrat	April 15, 1865	March 4, 1869	Completed Lincoln's Second Term	Office Vacant
Ulysses S. Grant	Republican	March 4, 1869	March 4, 1877	Two	Schuyler Colfax, Henry Wilson
Rutherford B. Hayes	Republican	March 3, 1877	March 4, 1881	One	William A. Wheeler
James A. Garfield	Republican	March 4, 1881	September 19, 1881	Died During First Term	Chester Arthur
Chester Arthur	Republican	September 20, 1881	March 4, 1885	Completed Garfield's Term	Office Vacant
Grover Cleveland	Democrat	March 4, 1885	March 4, 1889	One	Thomas A. Hendricks
Benjamin Harrison	Republican	March 4, 1889	March 4, 1893	One	Levi P. Morton
Grover Cleveland	Democrat	March 4, 1893	March 4, 1897	One	Adlai E. Stevenson
William McKinley	Republican	March 4, 1897	September 14, 1901	Served One Term, Died During Second Term	Garret A. Hobart, Theodore Roosevelt

PRESIDENT	PARTY	TOOK OFFICE	LEFT OFFICE	TERMS SERVED	VICE PRESIDENT
Theodore Roosevelt	Republican	September 14, 1901	March 4, 1909	Completed McKinley's Second Term, Served One Term	Office Vacant, Charles Fairbanks
William Taft	Republican	March 4, 1909	March 4, 1913	One	James S. Sherman
Woodrow Wilson	Democrat	March 4, 1913	March 4, 1921	Two	Thomas R. Marshall
Warren G. Harding	Republican	March 4, 1921	August 2, 1923	Died During First Term	Calvin Coolidge
Calvin Coolidge	Republican	August 3, 1923	March 4, 1929	Completed Harding's Term, Served One Term	Office Vacant, Charles Dawes
Herbert Hoover	Republican	March 4, 1929	March 4, 1933	One	Charles Curtis
Franklin D. Roosevelt	Democrat	March 4, 1933	April 12, 1945	Served Three Terms, Died During Fourth Term	John Nance Garner, Henry A. Wallace, Harry S. Truman
Harry S. Truman	Democrat	April 12, 1945	January 20, 1953	Completed Roosevelt's Fourth Term, Served One Term	Office Vacant, Alben Barkley
Dwight D. Eisenhower	Republican	January 20, 1953	January 20, 1961	Two	Richard Nixon
John F. Kennedy	Democrat	January 20, 1961	November 22, 1963	Died During First Term	Lyndon B. Johnson
Lyndon B. Johnson	Democrat	November 22, 1963	January 20, 1969	Completed Kennedy's Term, Served One Term	Office Vacant, Hubert H. Humphrey
Richard Nixon	Republican	January 20, 1969	August 9, 1974	Completed First Term, Resigned During Second Term	Spiro T. Agnew, Gerald Ford

PRESIDENT	PARTY	TOOK OFFICE	LEFT OFFICE	TERMS SERVED	VICE PRESIDENT
Gerald Ford	Republican	August 9, 1974	January 20, 1977	Completed Nixon's Second Term	Nelson A. Rockefeller
Jimmy Carter	Democrat	January 20, 1977	January 20, 1981	One	Walter Mondale
Ronald Reagan	Republican	January 20, 1981	January 20, 1989	Two	George H.W. Bush
George H.W. Bush	Republican	January 20, 1989	January 20, 1993	One	Dan Quayle
Bill Clinton	Democrat	January 20, 1993	January 20, 2001	Two	Al Gore
George W. Bush	Republican	January 20, 2001	January 20, 2009	Two	Dick Cheney
Barack Obama	Democrat	January 20, 2009			Joe Biden

"I am conscious that the position which I have been called to fill, though sufficient to satisfy the loftiest ambition, is surrounded by fearful responsibilities." Zachary Taylor

WRITE TO THE PRESIDENT

You may write to the president at:

**The White House
1600 Pennsylvania Avenue NW
Washington, DC 20500**

You may e-mail the president at:

comments@whitehouse.gov

GLOSSARY

administration - the people who manage a presidential government.

American Revolution - from 1775 to 1783. A war for independence between Great Britain and its North American colonies. The colonists won and created the United States of America.

annex - to take land and add it to a nation.

Confederate - relating to the Confederate States of America. This country was formed by the states of South Carolina, Georgia, Florida, Alabama, Louisiana, Mississippi, Texas, Virginia, Tennessee, Arkansas, and North Carolina when they left the Union between 1860 and 1861.

convention - a meeting of a political party's delegates to formulate a platform and select candidates for office.

debate - a contest in which two sides argue for or against something.

Democrat - a member of the Democratic political party. When Zachary Taylor was president, Democrats supported farmers and landowners.

Free-Soil - a political party that had power between 1848 and 1854. Its members opposed the extension of slavery into U.S. territories and the admission of slave states into the Union.

inauguration (ih-naw-gyuh-RAY-shuhn) - a ceremony in which a person is sworn into office.

neutral - not taking sides in a conflict.

running mate - a candidate running for a lower-rank position on an election ticket, especially the candidate for vice president.

secretary of state - a member of the president's cabinet who handles relations with other countries.

tutor - someone who teaches a student privately.

War of 1812 - from 1812 to 1814. A war fought between the United States and Great Britain over shipping rights and the capture of U.S. soldiers.

Whig - a member of a political party that was very strong in the early 1800s but ended in the 1850s. Whigs supported laws that helped business.

WEB SITES

To learn more about Zachary Taylor, visit ABDO Publishing Company on the World Wide Web at **www.abdopublishing.com**. Web sites about Zachary Taylor are featured on our Book Links page. These links are routinely monitored and updated to provide the most current information available.

INDEX